Learn SPANISH Through Fairy Tales

Beauty and the BEAST

Book Design & Production: Slangman Kids *(a division of Slangman Inc. and Slangman Publishing)*

Copy Editor: Julie Bobrick
Illustrated by: "Migs!" Sandoval
Translator: Marcela Redoles

Copyright © 2006 by David Burke

Published by: Slangman Kids *(a division of Slangman Inc. and Slangman Publishing)* 12206 Hillslope Street, Studio City, CA 91604 •USA • Toll Free Telephone from USA: 1-877-SLANGMAN (1-877-752-6462) • From outside the USA: 1-818-SLANGMAN (1-818-752-6462) • Worldwide Fax 1-413-647-1589 • Email: info@slangman.com • Website: www.slangman.com

"Migs!" Sandoval
✳ our illustrator ✳

Miguel *"Migs!"* Sandoval has been drawing cartoons since the age of 6 and has worked on numerous national commercials and movies as a sculptor, model builder, and illustrator. He was born in Los Angeles and was raised in a bilingual household, speaking English and Spanish. He currently lives in San Francisco where he is working on his new comic book series!

ISBN10: 1891888-862
ISBN13: 978189888-861
Printed in the U.S.A.

10 9 8 7 6 5 4 3 2 1

Order Form

Preview chapters & shop online!

www.slangman.com

SHIP TO: _____

_____

_____

Contact/Phone/Email: _____

SHIPPING

Domestic Orders

SURFACE MAIL
(Delivery time 5-7 business days).
Add $5 shipping/handling for the first item, $1.50 for each additional item.

RUSH SERVICE
Available at extra charge. Contact us for details.

International Orders

SURFACE MAIL
(Delivery time 6-8 weeks).
Add $6 shipping/handling for the first item, $2 for each additional item. Note that shipping to some countries may be more expensive. Contact us for details.

AIRMAIL (approx. 3-5 business days)
Available at extra charge. Contact us for details.

Method of Payment (Check one):

☐ Personal Check or Money Order
(Must be in U.S. funds and drawn on a U.S. bank.)

☐ VISA ☐ Master Card ☐ Discover ☐ American Express ☐ JCB

Credit Card Number

_____   ☐☐ ☐☐
Signature   Expiration Date

QTY	ISBN-13	TITLE	PRICE	LEVEL	TOTAL COST
English to CHINESE (Mandarin)					
	9781891888-793	Cinderella	$14.95	1	
	9781891888-854	Goldilocks	$14.95	2	
	9781891888-915	Beauty and the Beast	$14.95	3	
English to FRENCH					
	9781891888-755	Cinderella	$14.95	1	
	9781891888-816	Goldilocks	$14.95	2	
	9781891888-878	Beauty and the Beast	$14.95	3	
English to GERMAN					
	9781891888-762	Cinderella	$14.95	1	
	9781891888-830	Goldilocks	$14.95	2	
	9781891888-885	Beauty and the Beast	$14.95	3	
English to HEBREW					
	9781891888-922	Cinderella	$14.95	1	
	9781891888-939	Goldilocks	$14.95	2	
	9781891888-946	Beauty and the Beast	$14.95	3	
English to ITALIAN					
	9781891888-779	Cinderella	$14.95	1	
	9781891888 823	Goldilocks	$14.95	2	
	9781891888-892	Beauty and the Beast	$14.95	3	
English to JAPANESE					
	9781891888-786	Cinderella	$14.95	1	
	9781891888-847	Goldilocks	$14.95	2	
	9781891888-908	Beauty and the Beast	$14.95	3	
English to SPANISH					
	9781891888-748	Cinderella	$14.95	1	
	9781891888-809	Goldilocks	$14.95	2	
	9781891888-861	Beauty and the Beast	$14.95	3	
Japanese to ENGLISH 絵本で えいご を学ぼう					
	9781891888-038	Cinderella	$14.95	1	
	9781891888-045	Goldilocks	$14.95	2	
	9781891888-052	Beauty and the Beast	$14.95	3	
Korean to ENGLISH 동화를 통한 ENGLISH 배우기					
	9781891888-076	Cinderella	$14.95	1	
	9781891888-106	Goldilocks	$14.95	2	
	9781891888-113	Beauty and the Beast	$14.95	3	
Spanish to ENGLISH Aprende INGLÉS con cuentos de hadas					
	9781891888-953	Cinderella	$14.95	1	
	9781891888-960	Goldilocks	$14.95	2	
	9781891888-977	Beauty and the Beast	$14.95	3	

Total for Merchandise ☐

Sales Tax *(California residents only add applicable sales tax)* ☐

Shipping *(See left)* ☐

ORDER GRAND TOTAL ☐

Prices subject to change

SLANGMAN® KIDS

(a division of Slangman Publishing)

** TO PLACE AN ORDER - CALL, FAX, OR EMAIL: **
Phone: 1-818-752-6462 • Fax: 1-413-647-1589
Email: info@slangman.com • Web: www.slangman.com
12206 Hillslope Street • Studio City, CA 91604

(FORM 071606)

Dedication

The entire "Foreign Language Through Fairy Tales" series is dedicated to all the children of the world.

It is through their understanding, appreciation, and celebration of our differences that the world will become a better and safer place for us all.

One thing to remember...

The words in *green italics* throughout this fairy tale are words you've already learned in previous levels! Do you still remember what they mean?

1

hija →

mucho →

Once upon a time, there was a *papá* who had an eldest daughter named Julie, a middle **hija** named Tessa, and a youngest **hija** named Belle. He loved them very much. While preparing

to take a long trip, he asked each **hija**, "What can I bring you from my **viaje**?" "I'd like a ring to wear on my finger," said Julie. "I'd like a necklace to wear around my neck." said Tessa.

viaje

anillo

collar

3

Por favor ←

rosa ←

But Belle, who was the most *bonita* of all said, "Please. I don't want an **anillo** to wear on my finger or a **collar** to wear around my neck. All I want is a rose." He replied, "You shall each

4

receive your [gift]." "Oh, *Gracias! Gracias!*" → **regalo**

said each **hija**. Then their *papá* mounted

his [horse] as they shouted "Have a good → **caballo**

viaje, *papá!* We will miss you **mucho**!"

As he rode off, each **hija** shouted again,

"*Adiós, papá! Adiós!*" until he was out of sight.

Days later, it was time for him to return. So he

first stopped to buy an **anillo** for his eldest

6

hija to wear on her finger, a **collar** for his
second **hija** to wear around her neck, but
he waited to get closer to his *casa* to look
for a garden where he could find a **rosa** for

jardín

Belle. After a few hours, he saw a magnificent **jardín**. He got off his **caballo**, walked into the **jardín** and picked a **rosa** that was the most *bonita* he'd ever seen. At that very **momento**,

the *puerta* to the *casa* opened and a [beast] → **bestia**

came out and ran toward him. "Who stole

a **rosa** from my **jardín**?" exploded the

bestia. "Oh, **por favor**, [sir]!" said the → **señor**

papá. "**Por favor**, **señor**. Don't hurt me. I promised my **hija** that I'd bring her a **rosa** as a **regalo** after my long **viaje**. It was just ONE **rosa** from your **jardín**!" "It's still

stealing!" said the **bestia**. "I will spare your life if you bring me the **hija** you speak of by noon in six days. Here she will live the rest of her life." Naturally, the

mediodía

seis

papá was very upset by this request, but he promised to return with Belle at **mediodía** in **seis** days. As he arrived home, each **hija** rushed out to greet him. He gave them each

the **regalo** they'd asked for. Each **hija** was very *felíz* and shouted, "Oh, *gracias*, *papá*! *Gracias!*" "*De nada!*" he replied. But he was still upset because he had to tell Belle

13

te quiero ←

about the promise he'd made with the **bestia**.
"Belle, I love you. **Te quiero mucho**
and want you to be *felíz*. But I must tell you
what I have done…" Her *papá* went on to

explain what had happened that day and about
the promise he had made. He warned her about
how ugly the **bestia** was. But Belle felt
responsible because the **rosa** was a **regalo**

fea

she'd requested. So, she agreed to go. The days passed quickly until it was time to leave. As Belle and her *papá* mounted the **caballo** and rode off, she was very *triste* to say *adiós* to her sisters.

After a **viaje** that took several hours, Belle and her *papá* arrived at exactly **mediodía** as instructed. They got off the **caballo** and approached the *casa* of the **bestia**.

Hola ←

The *puerta* opened slowly and they walked in. "[Hello]!" said the *papá*. "¡**Hola**!" But there was no answer. Then they saw a *mesa* filled with food in the middle of the *cocina*.

It looked like someone was having a *fiesta*!

Just then they heard a deep voice say, "**Hola**.

This [lunch] is especially for you. **Por favor**,

enjoy!" Not wanting to be impolite, they began

almuerzo

19

eating the magnificent **almuerzo** before them. And so many desserts! Belle was so excited and already busily counting them. "...four, five, seis. And such wonderful desserts they were!

cuatro ←

cinco ←

She counted them again just to make sure,

"*Uno*, *dos*, *tres*, **cuatro**, **cinco**, **seis**! It

was true! **Seis** delicious desserts all for them!

They had never seen such a wonderful

almuerzo in their lives! Suddenly, they heard footsteps approaching. There he was – the **bestia** himself. Indeed, the **bestia** was truly **fea**. Scared, Belle said, "**Hola**,

señor and *gracias* for the delicious

almuerzo." "*De nada*," replied the **bestia**.

He seemed very kind toward Belle. Her → **amable**

papá was permitted to come visit her

every week which made her very *felíz*. He
gave Belle a kiss, mounted his **caballo**, and
said, "*Adiós*, Belle. **Te quiero**. **Te quiero
mucho**!" and rode off back to his *casa*.

At that very **momento**, the **bestia** turned toward Belle and said, "**Por favor**. What's mine is yours. I will return every day at **mediodía** to see you." He then quickly ran off, leaving Belle alone.

Because he was so **amable** toward her, Belle
was no longer afraid, and was even *felíz*
when he came to visit at **mediodía**. Every
day, they laughed more and more and enjoyed

sharing stories with each other in the **jardín**. But one day, the **bestia** didn't arrive at **mediodía** as usual, so Belle went to look for him. She walked outside into the **jardín** and there he was

lying on the ground lifeless. Belle cried, "Oh, why did you have to die, my **bestia**? **Te quiero**! **Te quiero mucho**!" She gave him a kiss on the cheek and suddenly right before her

 28

eyes, he awoke and was transformed into a *príncipe* who was very *guapo*, indeed! He explained to her that an evil magician had changed him into a **bestia** and only the kiss of

a *muchacha* who was truly in love with him could change him back to the *príncipe* he used to be. The next day at **mediodía**, Belle became his *esposa*, and they all lived happily ever after.